Presented to

Jamie Wastling

by Grandma & Grandpa Wastling

on 15th August 1999.

PRAYERS
for little hearts

Illustrated by Elena Kucharik

CANDLE
BOOKS

First published in the UK by Candle Books 1998
Distributed by STL, P.O. Box 300,
Carlisle, Cumbria, CA3 0QS.

Worldwide co-edition organised and produced by
Angus Hudson Ltd, Concorde House, Grenville Place, Mill Hill, London
NW7 3SA   Tel: +44 181 959 3668   Fax: +44 181 3678

ISBN 1-85985-189-4

Printed in Hong Kong

Prayer is a gift from God. God wants parents to pray for their children and with their children. He wants us to teach our children to pray. But when are children ready to learn about prayer? A simple guideline for parents is that as soon as children are able to talk, they are ready to pray. Certainly a child cannot grasp all that prayer means or everything that it does for us. But they can understand that prayer is simply talking to their heavenly Father.

God wants children to come to him in prayer:

When Jesus saw this, he was indignant. He said to them, "Let the little children come to me, and do not hinder them, for the kingdom of God belongs to such as these." (Mark 10:14)

God wants children to call him their heavenly Father:

> *This, then, is how you should pray: "Our Father in heaven, hallowed be your name." (Matthew 6:9)*

God wants children to make requests to him:

> *For everyone who asks receives; he who seeks finds; and to him who knocks, the door will be opened. (Matthew 7:8)*

God wants children to pray about any need:

> *Do not be anxious about anything, but in everything, by prayer and petition, with thanksgiving, present your requests to God. (Philippians 4:6)*

God wants children to pray every day:

> *Be joyful in hope, patient in affliction, faithful in prayer. (Romans 12:12)*

God wants children to pray at any time of the day:

Be joyful always; pray continually; give thanks in all circumstances, for this is God's will for you in Christ Jesus. (1 Thessalonians 5:16-18)

God wants all of his children to praise him:

Praise our God, all you his servants, you who fear him, both small and great! (Revelation 19:5)

All of the following prayers are based directly on verses from the Bible. Together with your child, you can look up the reference included with each prayer. It's never too early for little children to learn to pray. It's never too late for parents to start teaching their children to pray.

Dear God,

Please help me to love

you with all my heart and

with all my soul and with

all my strength.

In Jesus' name, Amen.

from Deuteronomy 6:5

Dear God,

You are very loving and
kind. You always keep your
promises. Please help me
to do my best for you.
In Jesus' name, Amen.

from 1 Kings 8:23

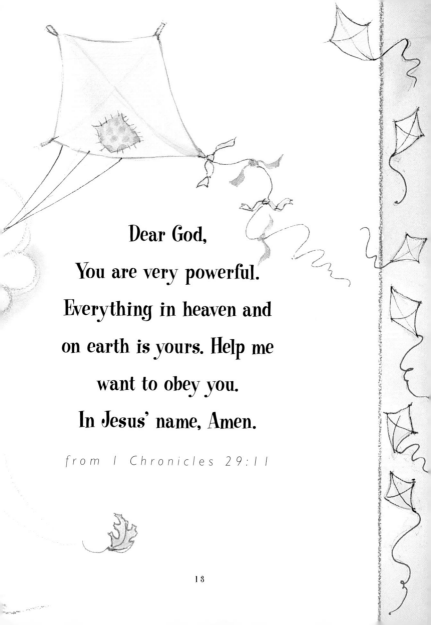

Dear God,

You are very powerful.
Everything in heaven and
on earth is yours. Help me
want to obey you.
In Jesus' name, Amen.

from 1 Chronicles 29:11

Dear God,

I want to pray to you

every day. Help me to pray

with all my heart.

In Jesus' name, Amen.

from Psalm 5:3

Dear God,
Help me to praise you
with all my heart. I want
to tell everyone about the
great things you do.
In Jesus' name, Amen.

from Psalm 9:1

Dear God,

I love you so much!

You have done so many

great things for me.

In Jesus' name, Amen.

from Psalm 18:1

Dear God,
Keep me from doing wrong
things on purpose. I want
my words and thoughts to
always please you.
In Jesus' name, Amen.

from Psalm 19:13-14

21

Dear God,

Create in me a new, clean
heart. Please fill my heart
with clean thoughts and
right desires.

In Jesus' name, Amen.

from Psalm 51:10

Dear God,

When I am afraid,

I will trust in you.

In Jesus' name, Amen.

from Psalm 56:3

Dear God,

You give me strength.

I will sing your praises

because you are my

place of safety.

In Jesus' name, Amen.

from Psalm 59:9

Dear God,
I will call to you when
trouble happens. Thank you
for being there to help.
In Jesus' name, Amen.

from Psalm 86:7

Dear God,

You made all the parts of

my body. Thank you for

making me so wonderfully!

In Jesus' name, Amen.

from Psalm 139:13-14

Dear God,

No one else is like you.

You are great, and your

name is full of power.

In Jesus' name, Amen.

from Jeremiah 10:6

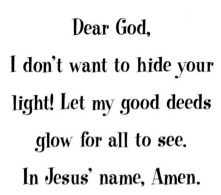

Dear God,
I don't want to hide your
light! Let my good deeds
glow for all to see.
In Jesus' name, Amen.

from Matthew 5:15-16

Dear God,

Please help me to treat
others the way I would
like them to treat me.
In Jesus' name, Amen.

from Matthew 7:12

Dear God,
Thank you for forgiving
my sins. Please help me to
forgive other people, too.
In Jesus' name, Amen.

from Mark 11:25

Dear God,
Oh, how I praise you!
I rejoice in God my Saviour!
In Jesus' name, Amen.

from Luke 1:46-47

Dear God,

Thank you for sending

Jesus to die so that we

can have eternal life.

In Jesus' name, Amen.

from John 3:16

43

Dear God,

Help me to love others just

as much as you love me.

In Jesus' name, Amen.

from John 13:34

Dear God,

Please help me not to get
tired of doing right. Help
me not to give up.
In Jesus' name, Amen.

from Galatians 6:9

Dear God,
Show me how to honour my
father and mother. Please
help me to obey them.
In Jesus' name, Amen.

from Ephesians 6:1-2

Dear God,

Please help me to stay

away from complaining

and arguing.

In Jesus' name, Amen.

from Philippians 2:14

Dear God,

Help me not to worry
about anything but to pray
about everything.
In Jesus' name, Amen.

from Philippians 4:6

Dear God,
Help me to trust you for
the problems I face each
day. Help me to grow
closer to you.
In Jesus' name, Amen.

from Colossians 2:6

Dear God,

Help me to always be

joyful. Help me to always

keep on praying.

In Jesus' name, Amen.

from I Thessalonians 5:16-17

Dear God,

Thank you that we can

ask you for wisdom. Please

give me a lot of it.

In Jesus' name, Amen.

from James 1:5

Dear God,

Please help me to be a good

listener. Help me not to

become angry with others.

In Jesus' name, Amen.

from James 1:19

Dear God,
Help me to learn more
and more about Jesus.
In Jesus' name, Amen.

from 2 Peter 3:18

Dear God,

Help me to really love

people. Help me to prove

it with my actions.

In Jesus' name, Amen.

from I John 3:18

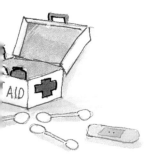

Dear God Almighty,
You are worthy to receive
glory and honour and power.
You have created all things.
In Jesus' name, Amen.

from Revelation 4:11

Prayers for
Special Days

With everything else parents have to do to
prepare for special occasions, we can miss the
opportunity to help point out God's blessings in
our children's lives. In the Old Testament God
directed the nation of Israel to build an altar or
offer a sacrifice on special occasions. Today God
is pleased when his people honour him with
prayers of thanks for the special events in their
lives. Praying with our children on their special
days help them understand that all good things
come from God. Here are some prayers for
special days.

BIRTHDAY

Dear God,

Thank you for letting me
be born. Thank you for
giving me life. Thank you
for another birthday. Help
me to live for you.
In Jesus' name, Amen.

Dear God,

Thank you for all the presents that people give us at Christmas. And thank you for giving Jesus to us as the best gift of all.

In Jesus' name, Amen.

Dear God,

I'm sad that Jesus died on
the cross to pay for sin.
But I'm glad that he paid
for my sin. Thank you for
raising him to life again!
In Jesus' name, Amen.

THANKSGIVING

Dear God,

Thank you for giving me

food, clothes, and a place

to live. Thank you for my

family and relatives. Please

help me to be more thankful

on other days, too.

In Jesus' name, Amen.

MOTHER'S DAY

Dear God,

Thank you for my mum.

Please give her a good day.

Please help me to love and

obey her all the time.

In Jesus' name, Amen.

FATHER'S DAY

Dear God,

Thank you for my dad.

Please give him a good day.

Please help me to love and

obey him all the time.

In Jesus' name, Amen.

Dear God,

Thank you for Grandma and

Grandpa. They are special

to me. Thank you that I am

special to them, too. Please

take care of them.

In Jesus' name, Amen.

Dear God,

Thank you for my new

school. Help me not to be

afraid. Please help my

teacher to help me learn

and grow.

In Jesus' name, Amen.

Dear God,

Thank you that I got to

meet a new friend today.

Help me to be a good friend.

Thank you for being a

friend to us.

In Jesus' name, Amen.

Taking a Trip

Dear God,

Thank you that we are

able to go on this special trip.

Please keep us safe as we

travel. Help us to get

along as a family.

In Jesus' name, Amen.